This book offers an extensive selection of kid-friendly recipes for dinner. From classic comfort foods to creative new flavor combinations, you'll find something that's sure to please every taste bud. You'll also get plenty of ideas on how to customize recipes and make them healthier too! Prepare tasty meals quickly with time-saving tips and tricks that will have dinner on the table in no time. With these simple recipes, your kids will love coming home to a delicious, nutritious meal that you both can enjoy together. Enjoy preparing easy dinners for family night with this collection of scrumptious kid-approved dishes!

Bon appetite!

Fish And Chips

Ingredients

900 g potatoes.
sunflower oil , for deep-frying.
225 g white fish fillets , skin off, pin-boned, from sustainable sources.
225 g plain flour , plus extra for dusting.
285 ml cold beer.
3 heaped teaspoons baking powder.
MUSHY PEAS.
a few sprigs of fresh mint.

Fish and chips is a classic dish that's loved by many! With just a few simple ingredients, you can easily make this healthy and easy dinner for kids. Here's how to get it done:

1. Start off by preheating the oven to 190°C/375°F/gas 5. Peel the potatoes, then cut into thick chips. Parboil the chips in boiling salted water for 5-7 minutes, depending on how thick they are. Drain and leave to steam dry while you prepare the fish and batter.

2. Put the flour, baking powder and beer in a large bowl and whisk together until smooth. Dust the fish fillets with a little extra flour, then dip in the batter to coat.

3. Heat the oil in a deep-fat fryer or large saucepan until it reaches 180°C/350°F on a cooking thermometer. Carefully place the chips into the hot fat and fry for 10 minutes or until golden. Drain well on kitchen paper.

4. Reheat the oil until it reaches 190°C/375°F on a cooking thermometer, then deep-fry the fish in batches for 5 minutes or until cooked through and golden. Drain well on kitchen paper and season with salt while still hot.

5. Place the chips onto a baking tray, then cook for 15-20 minutes in the preheated oven until crisp. Serve with the fish and mushy peas, and garnish with fresh mint leaves if desired. Enjoy!

Fish and chips is a great dish to make at home, offering delicious flavors and a healthy dinner option for the whole family. With just a few ingredients, it's easy to whip up in no time. Enjoy!

Bagel Pizzas

Ingredients

4 full-sized plain bagels, halved.
1/2 cup store-bought or homemade pizza sauce.
8 ounces shredded mozzarella cheese.
4 ounces mini pepperoni.
Dried basil, for garnish.

Making bagel pizzas is an easy and healthy dinner for kids. To prepare, preheat your oven to 375°F and line a baking sheet with parchment paper. Place the bagel halves on the baking sheet and spread each half with pizza sauce. Sprinkle mozzarella cheese onto each one and top with mini pepperonis. Bake in preheated oven for 12-15 minutes or until the cheese is melted and bubbly. Sprinkle with a touch of dried basil before serving. Enjoy your delicious bagel pizza!

This is an easy and nutritious way to get your kids excited about dinner! Making bagel pizzas gives you the opportunity to involve them in the process, from assembling ingredients to baking. Plus, they'll love how delicious their creations turn out! You can even customize each pizza with different toppings according to everyone's tastes.

Mac And Cheese

Ingredients

8 ounces uncooked elbow macaroni.
¼ cup salted butter.
3 tablespoons all-purpose flour. Great Value All-Purpose Flour, 5LB. ...
2 ½ cups milk, or more as needed.
2 cups shredded sharp Cheddar cheese.
½ cup finely grated Parmesan cheese. ...
salt and ground black pepper to taste (Optional)

Making macaroni and cheese is a healthy and easy dinner for kids, as it is an excellent source of calcium and protein. With the right ingredients, you can make this classic dish in minutes.

To get started, bring a large pot of salted water to a boil over high heat. Add 8 ounces of uncooked elbow macaroni, and cook until al dente (about 7 minutes). Drain the cooked pasta in a colander.

Meanwhile, melt ¼ cup of salted butter in a large saucepan over medium heat. Add 3 tablespoons of all-purpose flour to the melted butter, stirring constantly until the mixture thickens slightly and becomes a paste. Slowly add 2 ½ cups of milk to the saucepan, continually stirring until fully incorporated and thickened.

Remove the pan from heat and stir in 2 cups of shredded sharp Cheddar cheese, ½ cup of finely grated Parmesan cheese, and salt and ground black pepper to taste (optional). Add the cooked macaroni to the saucepan and mix until all of the pasta is evenly coated.

Serve the macaroni and cheese hot, with extra Parmesan cheese sprinkled on top if desired. Enjoy!

Beef Tacos

Ingredients

1 lb lean ground beef
1 medium onion, chopped
1 teaspoon chili powder
1/2 teaspoon salt
1/2 teaspoon garlic powder
1 can (8 oz) tomato sauce
1 box (4.6 oz) Old El Paso™ Crunchy Taco Shells (12 Count)
1 1/2 cups shredded Cheddar cheese (6 oz)
2 cups shredded lettuce
2 medium tomatoes, chopped
3/4 cup Old El Paso™ Thick 'n Chunky salsa
3/4 cup sour cream, if desired

Beef tacos are a healthy and easy dinner for kids. With just a few simple ingredients, you can whip up a tasty taco meal in no time! To get started, brown the ground beef with the onion in a large skillet over medium heat. Once it's cooked through, add chili powder, salt and garlic powder to the ground beef. Stir in the tomato sauce and let it simmer for 5 minutes. To prepare the tacos, heat up a taco shell according to package instructions. Fill each taco shell with the beef mixture and top with cheese, lettuce, tomatoes and salsa. Finish off your tacos with a dollop of sour cream if desired! Serve this yummy treat for dinner tonight and watch how quickly your kids devour it. Bon appetit!

Baked Potato Bar

Ingredients

5 pounds baked potatoes.
3-5 pounds pulled pork cooked.
2 cups sharp cheddar cheese shredded.
1/2 pound bacon cooked & crumbled.
1 cup sour cream.
1/2 cup chives chopped.
2 cups broccoli cooked.
1 bottle bbq sauce.

A baked potato bar is an easy and healthy dinner option for kids, and it's simple to prepare. Start by baking five pounds of potatoes according to the instructions on the package. While they're cooking, pre-cook three to five pounds of pulled pork as well as one-half pound of bacon. Once the potatoes are done, split them open and sprinkle two cups of shredded sharp cheddar cheese over the top. Then, add the cooked pulled pork, crumbled bacon, one cup of sour cream, half a cup of chopped chives and two cups of cooked broccoli. Finally, make sure to provide some BBQ sauce for everyone to enjoy. With minimal effort, you can create a delicious and nutritious baked potato bar that all the kids will love! Enjoy!

Meatball Spaghetti

Ingredients
3 slices white bread, (crusts removed), diced or torn to
pieces.
2/3 cup cold water.
1 lb lean ground beef, (7%-15% fat)
1 lb Sweet Ground Italian sausage, casings removed.
1/4 cup grated parmesan cheese, plus more to serve.
4 cloves garlic, minced.
1 tsp sea salt.
1/2 tsp black pepper.

Meatball spaghetti is a delicious, healthy and easy dinner for kids that can be prepared in no time. To make this dish start by preheating the oven to 350°F. Then, in a medium bowl, combine the diced bread and water and let it sit for 3 minutes before adding the ground beef, sausage, parmesan cheese, garlic, salt and pepper. Mix together until all ingredients are evenly distributed. After that, form 1 ½ inch balls of the meatball mixture and place them on a lightly greased baking sheet. Bake for 20-25 minutes or until the internal temperature reaches 165°F. Once done, serve over spaghetti with extra parmesan cheese if desired. Enjoy!

Chicken Tortellini

Ingredients

2 tablespoons olive oil.
8 oz boneless skinless chicken breast, cut into 1/4-inch slices.
3 cups fresh small broccoli florets.
2 teaspoons chopped garlic.
1 1/2 cups Progresso™ chicken broth (from 32-oz carton)
2 packages (9 oz each) refrigerated cheese tortellini.
1 cup milk.

Preparing a healthy and easy dinner for the kids doesn't have to be a hassle. This delicious Chicken Tortellini is sure to please everyone at the table.

To make this dish, start by heating two tablespoons of olive oil in a large skillet over medium-high heat. Once it's hot, add the chicken slices and cook for about 4 minutes until they're no longer pink. Add the broccoli florets, garlic, and a pinch of salt, then cook for another 3 to 4 minutes.

Next, pour in the Progresso™ chicken broth and bring it to a boil over high heat. Once boiling, add the tortellini and cook for about 8 minutes until the pasta is cooked through. Then, reduce the heat to low and stir in the milk. Simmer for a few more minutes until it thickens up a bit. Taste and season with salt and pepper if needed.

Serve the tortellini with some extra grated Parmesan cheese on top. Enjoy! This Chicken Tortellini is a healthy and delicious dinner that your kids are sure to love. It's quick and easy, ready in just 30 minutes. Enjoy!

*Note: You can customize this dish with other vegetables like mushrooms, bell peppers or spinach. For added protein, you can also add shrimp or cooked sausage. Enjoy!

Enjoy! With its delicious flavor and simple preparation, this Chicken Tortellini is a surefire winner for any family dinner. It's the perfect healthy and easy dinner for kids - ready in just 30 minutes! Bon appetit!

Gnocchi With Sausage

Ingredients
15 oz Italian sausage spicy, crumbled.
16 oz potato gnocchi.
½ cup chicken broth.
1 cup heavy cream.
4 cloves garlic minced.
½ teaspoon Italian seasoning or Herbs from Provence.
13 oz tomato sauce such as tomato pasta sauce or
marinara.
5 oz spinach fresh.

This delicious and easy gnocchi with sausage dish is perfect for a healthy dinner for kids. To prepare, start by heating a large skillet to medium heat and adding the crumbled Italian sausage. Cook until lightly browned. Remove from skillet and set aside.

Add the gnocchi to boiling salted water in a pot over high heat. Cook for 3 minutes or until they float to the top of the water, then drain and set aside.

In the same skillet you cooked the sausage in, add chicken broth and bring it to a boil. Add heavy cream, garlic, Italian seasoning or Herbs from Provence and reduce heat to low. Slowly stir in tomato sauce and cooked sausage until the mixture is heated through.

Stir in spinach until wilted and combine with gnocchi to finish. This tasty dish is sure to be a hit with kids and adults alike! Enjoy!

Chicken Quesadillas

Ingredients

1 pound skinless, boneless chicken breast, diced.
1 (1.27 ounce) packet fajita seasoning.
1 tablespoon vegetable oil.
2 green bell peppers, chopped.
2 red bell peppers, chopped.
1 onion, chopped. ...
10 (10 inch) flour tortillas.
1 (8 ounce) package shredded Cheddar cheese.

Chicken quesadillas make for a healthy and easy dinner for the whole family. To start preparing, dice the boneless chicken breasts and season with fajita seasoning. In a large skillet over medium heat, heat vegetable oil and add in the diced chicken breast, green bell peppers, red bell peppers, and onions. Cook until vegetables are softened and chicken is cooked through. To assemble the quesadillas, place about ¼ cup of cheese onto one side of a tortilla. Top with cooked vegetables and chicken, then add another ¼ cup of cheese to the top. Fold over into a half-moon shape and cook in a skillet on medium-high heat until golden brown. Repeat this process with the remaining tortillas. Serve warm and enjoy!

For a fun variation, try adding black beans to the quesadillas or swapping out Cheddar cheese for Monterey Jack. Using flavorful ingredients like jalapenos, salsa, and guacamole can also liven up this classic dish. Chicken quesadillas make for a healthy and delicious dinner that can be customized to fit the tastes of any family. Enjoy!

Sesame Chicken Meatballs

Ingredients

1 pound ground chicken.
½ cup breadcrumbs.
2 tablespoons soy sauce.
1 tablespoon Shaoxing wine (or mirin)
½ tablespoon sesame oil.
1 tablespoon ginger, freshly grated.
½ teaspoon garlic powder.
2 tablespoons green onions, finely chopped.

These chicken sesame meatballs are a healthy and easy dinner option that your kids will love. To prepare the meatballs, simply combine all of the ingredients in a large bowl and mix together until everything is well-incorporated. Once the mixture is ready, form it into small balls with your hands. Place them on a parchment paper-lined baking sheet, and bake at 350°F for about 20 minutes or until the meatballs are cooked through. Serve hot with a side of your favorite vegetables or salad. Enjoy!

This is an easy recipe that requires minimal preparation time, making it perfect for busy weeknights. Plus, you can use leftover meatballs as a quick and simple lunch the next day. So when you're looking for a healthy dinner option that your kids will love, give these chicken sesame meatballs a try!

Chicken Noodle Casserole

Ingredients
12 oz. wide egg noodles.
10.5-oz. cans cream of chicken soup.
1 c. whole milk.
1 c. shredded sharp cheddar cheese.
1 tsp. ground black pepper.
1/2 tsp. kosher salt.
3 c. cooked, shredded chicken (from 1 rotisserie chicken)
1/2. small yellow onion, finely chopped.

Making a chicken noodle casserole is an easy and healthy dinner option for kids. To begin, preheat your oven to 400 degrees Fahrenheit. In a large pot over medium heat, cook the egg noodles according to package directions. Drain the cooked noodles and set aside.

In a medium-sized bowl, combine the cream of chicken soup, milk, shredded cheese, ground black pepper and kosher salt. Stir until the ingredients are completely blended.

In a 9-by-13-inch baking dish, spread the cooked egg noodles. Top with the shredded chicken and onion pieces. Pour the cream of chicken mixture over the noodles and chicken, spreading evenly to ensure everything is coated.

Bake for 25 minutes until the cheese is melted and bubbly. Let cool for about 10 minutes before serving. Enjoy!

This chicken noodle casserole provides a comforting, delicious and healthy dinner option for kids. It's quick to prepare, full of flavor and sure to please everyone at the table.

Chicken Tacos

Ingredients

¼ cup olive oil.
2 medium yellow onions, finely chopped.
2 bell peppers (any color), finely chopped.
4 cloves garlic, finely chopped.
2 pounds ground chicken (not extra-lean all breast meat)
1 tablespoon paprika.
2 teaspoons ancho chili powder.
1½ teaspoons ground cumin.

Preparing chicken tacos is a healthy and easy dinner option that kids will love. To make them, begin by heating ¼ cup of olive oil in a large skillet over medium-high heat. Add in chopped onions and bell peppers, as well as the minced garlic, stirring everything until it's lightly browned and fragrant.

Then, add in the ground chicken, breaking it up with a spoon as you stir. Once the chicken is cooked through, sprinkle in paprika, ancho chili powder and cumin. Stir everything to combine and let it cook for 3-4 minutes until all of the flavors have melded together.

Once done, serve your chicken tacos with tortillas, your favorite toppings and a side dish. Enjoy!

This is an easy yet tasty way to whip up a healthy dinner for the kids!

By following these easy steps, you can have a delicious batch of chicken tacos ready in no time. Not only are they healthy and delicious, but your kids will love them too! Try it out today for a quick and tasty dinner option.

Enjoy!

Chicken Noodle Soup

Ingredients
2 tablespoons unsalted butter.
1 onion, diced.
2 carrots, peeled and diced.
2 celery ribs, diced.
3 cloves garlic, minced.
8 cups chicken stock.
2 bay leaves.
Kosher salt freshly ground black
pepper, to taste.

Chicken noodle soup is a delicious, healthy and easy dinner option for kids. To prepare it, start by melting the butter over medium heat in a large pot. Add the onion, carrots and celery to the pot and cook until softened, about 5 minutes. Stir in garlic until fragrant, about 1 minute. Pour in chicken stock, bay leaves, salt and pepper. Bring the soup to a boil. Reduce heat and simmer for 15 minutes or until the vegetables are tender. Finally, add noodles and cook according to package instructions. Serve hot with your favorite toppings such as shredded cheese, croutons or chopped parsley. Enjoy!

Chicken Pot Pie

Making a homemade chicken pot pie is an easy and healthy dinner option for kids. To prepare this delicious dish, you will need 1 pound of skinless, boneless chicken breast halves - cubed, 1 cup sliced carrots, 1 cup frozen green peas, ½ cup sliced celery, ⅓ cup butter, ⅓ cup chopped onion, ⅓ cup all-purpose flour, and ½ teaspoon of Great Value Iodized Salt.

To begin, preheat your oven to 375°F. In a large skillet, melt the butter over medium heat. Add the onion and celery to the melted butter and cook until they are soft and tender. Once done, add in the cubed chicken and cook until it is no longer pink. Add the carrots, peas and salt to the skillet, stirring occasionally for about 5 minutes.

In a small bowl combine flour with ¼ cup of cold water until it forms a paste-like consistency. Gradually add this flour mixture to the skillet, stirring constantly. Cook for an additional 2 minutes or until the mixture thickens.

Pour the filling into a 9-inch deep-dish pie plate and spread it evenly across the bottom of the dish. Place your pie crust over top of the filling and cut four slits in it with a sharp knife.

Bake for 40 to 45 minutes or until the crust is golden brown. Let it cool for 5 to 10 minutes before serving. Enjoy this delicious and easy-to-make chicken pot pie with your family!

This dish can be served along with a side of roasted vegetables, mashed potatoes or a simple green salad for a complete meal. Try adding other favorite ingredients to the filling for even more flavor. With just a few ingredients and some hands-on time, you can create this healthy and delicious dinner for your kids to enjoy!

Tuna Pasta

Ingredients

2 tablespoons olive oil.
2 large cloves garlic minced.
1 (5 ounce) can tuna, drained I prefer tuna
packed in oil.
1 teaspoon lemon juice.
1 tablespoon fresh parsley chopped.
Salt & pepper to taste.
4 ounces uncooked pasta (I used spaghetti)

Tuna pasta is a healthy and easy dinner idea for kids. With just 6
ingredients, it's an inexpensive yet delicious meal that the whole
family can enjoy!

To start preparing this tasty dish, begin by heating olive oil in a large
skillet over medium heat. Add minced garlic and sauté for about 1
minute or until fragrant. Add the drained tuna and lemon juice,
stirring to combine all ingredients. Cook for a couple of minutes until
everything is heated through.

Once cooked, stir in the freshly chopped parsley, adding salt and
pepper to taste. Meanwhile, cook your chosen pasta according to
package instructions. Once cooked, drain the pasta and add it to the
skillet with the tuna mixture. Stir to combine, and you're done!

Tuna pasta is an easy, delicious dinner for kids that can be on the
table in just 15 minutes. Enjoy!

Enjoy your homemade tuna pasta and bon appetit!

Chicken Alfredo

Ingredients

1 tbsp olive oil.
4 skinless boneless chicken thighs, cut in half.
300g fettuccine, or tagliatelle.
1 tbsp butter.
200ml double cream.
½ a nutmeg, grated.
100g parmesan.
parsley, chopped, to serve.

Chicken Alfredo is a delicious and easy dish to make for dinner. It's also a great, healthy option for kids! To prepare Chicken Alfredo, start by heating the olive oil in a large pan over medium heat. Add the chicken thighs and cook for about 5 minutes until golden brown on both sides. Remove the chicken from the pan and set aside. Now add the butter to the pan and let it melt. Add the cream, grated nutmeg and parmesan and bring to a simmer, stirring occasionally until thickened. Return the chicken to the pan and heat through for 2-3 minutes, then toss in your cooked pasta or tagliatelle. Serve with chopped parsley and a sprinkle of parmesan, if desired. Enjoy your delicious Chicken Alfredo!

Baked Salmon With Potatoes

Ingredients
Potatoes.
Olive oil.
Salmon fillets.
Butter.
Lemon juice.
Dijon mustard.
Kosher salt.
Black pepper.

This healthy and easy dinner for kids is an ideal recipe to try out. To prepare this delicious baked salmon with potatoes, preheat your oven to 400°F and line a baking sheet with parchment paper.

Cut the potatoes into 1/2-inch thick slices and arrange them in a single layer on the baking sheet. Drizzle the potatoes with olive oil and bake for 20 minutes.

Remove the baking sheet from the oven and place salmon fillets on top of the potatoes. Spread butter over each piece of salmon and season with lemon juice, Dijon mustard, kosher salt, and black pepper. Place back in the oven and bake for an additional 15-20 minutes, until the potatoes are golden brown and the salmon is cooked through.

Serve the baked salmon with potatoes hot, right out of the oven. Enjoy!

Lasagna Bolognese

Ingredients

2 ounces diced pancetta, finely chopped.
1 medium Spanish onion or yellow onion, finely chopped.
1 rib celery, finely chopped.
1 carrot, finely chopped.
4 tablespoons unsalted butter.
11 ounces ground beef.
4 ounces ground pork.
4 ounces ground Italian sausage.

Lasagna bolognese is a classic Italian dish that makes for an easy and healthy dinner for the whole family. Preparing this delicious meal is relatively simple and requires just a few ingredients.

To start, you will need 2 ounces of diced pancetta, chopped finely; one medium onion, either Spanish or yellow, chopped finely; one rib of celery, chopped finely; and one carrot, also chopped finely.

Next, add 4 tablespoons of unsalted butter to a large skillet or pot over medium heat. Once melted, add the diced pancetta and sauté for about 5 minutes until browned and fragrant.

Afterwards, add the onion, celery and carrot to the skillet. Sauté together for another 5 minutes until vegetables are softened and lightly browned.

Finally, add 11 ounces ground beef, 4 ounces ground pork, and 4 ounces of Italian sausage to the pan. Cook together until the meat is fully cooked through.

Now your lasagna bolognese is ready to use as a filling for your lasagna dish. Enjoy!

Shrimp Pasta

Ingredients

8 ounces fettuccine.
1 pound medium shrimp, peeled and deveined.
Kosher salt and freshly ground black pepper, to taste.
8 tablespoons 1 stick unsalted butter, divided.
4 cloves garlic, minced.
½ teaspoon dried oregano.
½ teaspoon crushed red pepper flakes.
2 cups baby arugula.

Shrimp Pasta is a healthy and easy dinner for kids that you can whip up in no time. To prepare it, start by bringing a large pot of salted water to a boil over high heat. Once boiling, add the fettuccine and cook until al dente according to package directions. Drain pasta into a colander and set aside.

Meanwhile, in a large skillet over medium heat, melt 4 tablespoons of butter. Add the shrimp and season with salt and pepper to taste. Cook, stirring occasionally until pink and cooked through, about 3-4 minutes; set aside.

To the same skillet add remaining butter, garlic, oregano and red pepper flakes. Cook, stirring frequently, until fragrant, about 1-2 minutes. Stir in the cooked pasta and shrimp; season with salt and pepper to taste.

Finally, stir in the arugula until wilted, about 1 minute. Serve immediately, garnished with more red pepper flakes if desired. Enjoy!

Steak And Lemon Mashed Potatoes

INGREDIENTS

1 1/2 lb. Yukon gold potatoes, peeled and cut into
2-inch chunks.
Kosher salt and freshly ground black pepper.
1 c. fresh or frozen peas.
2 tsp. lemon zest plus 2 tablespoons juice.
3 tbsp. olive oil, divided.
2 (3/4-inch-thick) strip steaks (about 1 1/2
pounds total)
2 small shallots, thinly sliced.
1/2 c.

This easy and healthy dinner for kids combines steak and mashed potatoes. To prepare, start by preheating your oven to 375°F. Place the peeled and cubed Yukon gold potatoes in a pot of boiling salted water and cook for about 20 minutes until tender. Drain the potatoes and return them to the pot over low heat, stirring to evaporate any excess moisture. Mash the potatoes with a fork or potato masher until smooth, then season liberally with salt and pepper to taste.

Next, heat two tablespoons of olive oil in a skillet over medium-high heat. Season both sides of the strip steaks liberally with salt and pepper. Add the steak to the pan and cook for about 4 minutes per side, or until cooked to your desired doneness. Remove the steak from the pan and set aside to rest.

In the same skillet, heat one tablespoon of olive oil over medium-low heat. Add the shallots and cook for several minutes until softened. Then add in the peas, lemon zest, and lemon juice. Cook for an additional three to four minutes, or until the peas are softened.

Divide the mashed potatoes among plates and top with steak and the shallot-pea mixture. Serve hot. Enjoy!

Pepperoni Pizza

Ingredients

Pizza dough (store bought or homemade
pizza dough, let rise on a counter 2+ hours in
advance)
Flour (for stretching the dough)
Olive oil.
Pizza sauce.
Shredded mozzarella cheese (I prefer full fat
mozzarella cheese)
Pepperoni slices.
Parmesan cheese.

Pepperoni pizza is a classic favorite that can be made easily and quickly for a
healthy and delicious dinner. Here's how to make your own pepperoni pizza
at home:

1. First, prepare the dough by either buying pre-made dough from the store or
making your own with flour, water, salt, sugar and yeast. Make sure to let the
dough rise for at least two hours before you start assembling the pizza.

2. When you're ready to assemble, spread a thin layer of olive oil on a baking
sheet and place the dough in it. Then sprinkle some flour over the dough and
use your hands to stretch it into a round shape that's about 12-14 inches in
diameter.

3. Spread your pizza sauce over the dough, leaving a one-inch gap around the
edge. Top with mozzarella cheese and a generous helping of pepperoni slices.
Finally, top with grated parmesan cheese and any other desired toppings.

4. Bake at 425 degrees Fahrenheit for 20 minutes, or until the cheese is
melted and bubbling. Slice into wedges, serve hot and enjoy!

Making your own pepperoni pizza at home is a healthy and easy dinner
option that kids love. Enjoy this classic favorite with friends and family!

Sausage And Cheese Lasagna

Ingredients

1 pound Bob Evans Italian Roll Sausage.
1 jar pasta sauce (26 oz)
1 can tomato sauce (15 oz)
1 package oven ready lasagna noodles (8 oz)
1 container ricotta cheese (15 oz)
1 teaspoon Italian seasoning.
4 cups shredded mozzarella cheese.

This delicious sausage and cheese lasagna is the perfect meal for a healthy, easy dinner with kids. To prepare it, start by preheating your oven to 375 degrees Fahrenheit. In a large skillet over medium heat, cook the Bob Evans Italian Roll Sausage until it is lightly browned and cooked through. Drain any excess grease from the cooked sausage and set aside.

Next, in a large bowl mix together the pasta sauce, tomato sauce, Italian seasoning and ricotta cheese until it is well combined. Layer half of the lasagna noodles in the bottom of a 9x13 inch baking dish that has been lightly sprayed with cooking spray. Spread half of the sausage mixture over the noodles and spread half of the cheese mixture over the sausage.

Sprinkle 2 cups of mozzarella cheese over the top, and then layer the remaining lasagna noodles over the cheese. Top these with the remaining sausage mixture, followed by the rest of the cheese sauce. Finally, sprinkle on another 2 cups of shredded mozzarella cheese.

Cover the dish with aluminum foil and bake it in the preheated oven for 30 minutes. Uncover the dish and continue baking for an additional 15 minutes, or until the cheese is melted and lightly browned. Allow to cool before serving. Enjoy!

Grilled Hot Dogs

Grilled hot dogs are a classic summer cookout favorite. They're also an easy and healthy dinner option for kids. Preparing grilled hot dogs is super simple - all you need to do is gather the ingredients, heat up your grill, and get cooking!

To prepare grilled hot dogs, you'll need eight hot dogs, ¼ cup ketchup, 2 Tbsp Worcestershire Sauce, 1 minced garlic clove, and 1 tsp of vegetable oil. Start by preheating the grill to medium-high heat. Once it's hot enough, place the hot dogs on the grill and cook for about 8 minutes or until browned and cooked through.

In a small bowl, mix together the ketchup, Worcestershire sauce, garlic and vegetable oil. Brush the hot dogs with the mixture when they come off of the grill. Serve with your favorite condiments and sides for a delicious summer meal! Enjoy!

Cornflake Chicken

Making Cornflake Chicken is a healthy and easy dinner for kids. It is simple to prepare, only requiring some milk, an egg, flour, garlic powder, salt and pepper, cornflakes and chicken breasts.

To begin preparing your meal, stir the milk, egg, flour, garlic powder, salt and pepper together in a bowl. Then take a chicken breast and dredge it in the milk mixture and roll it in the cornflakes to coat. Place on a baking sheet or dish, and bake for 45 minutes until the juices run clear and no longer pink at the bone.

Enjoy your delicious Cornflake Chicken! It's sure to be a hit with the kids!

This meal is a great option for busy evenings when time is of the essence. It's nutritious and tasty, so everyone will be looking forward to dinner. With this easy-to-follow recipe, you can make Cornflake Chicken in no time!

Happy cooking!

French Onion Soup

Ingredients

6 large red or yellow onions (about 3 pounds)
4 tablespoons extra virgin olive oil.
2 tablespoons butter.
1 teaspoon sugar.
Kosher salt.
2 cloves garlic, minced.
8 cups beef stock, chicken stock, or a combination of
the two.
1/2 cup dry vermouth or dry white wine.

French Onion Soup is a delicious and healthy dinner option that is easy to prepare, making it perfect for busy families. To make the soup, start by slicing the onions into thin rings and sautéing them in butter and olive oil over low heat until they are lightly browned and softened. Next, add the garlic, sugar, and salt and cook for another few minutes. Pour the beef or chicken stock (or a combination of both) and vermouth into the pot, stirring until everything is combined. Bring the soup to a boil and then reduce the heat to low and simmer for 30-45 minutes before serving. This hearty soup can be served with some crusty bread or a topping of melted cheese. French Onion Soup is an easy and healthy dinner that kids love - plus, it's a great way to use up all those onions in your pantry!

This recipe can be easily adapted to make a vegetarian version by replacing the beef or chicken stock with vegetable broth. You can also adjust the salt level to your taste and add other herbs and spices for flavor. Enjoy!

Tomato Soup

Ingredients

1-1.25kg/2lb 4oz-2lb 12oz ripe tomatoes.
1 medium onion.
1 small carrot.
1 celery stick.
2 tbsp olive oil.
2 squirts of tomato purée (about 2 tsp)
a good pinch of sugar.
2 bay leaves.

Making tomato soup is an easy and healthy dinner option that kids love! To make it, start by prepping the ingredients. Peel and dice the onion, carrot, and celery. Cut the tomatoes into wedges. Heat up the olive oil in a large saucepan over medium heat. Add all of the diced vegetables, then add in the tomato purée and sugar. Stir until everything is combined and the vegetables are softened. Add in the tomato wedges and bay leaves, then cover with a lid. Let it simmer for 25-35 minutes until all of the vegetables are cooked through and soft. When finished, remove the bay leaves, then use an immersion blender to puree the soup until it's smooth. Serve warm with a sprinkle of fresh herbs, and enjoy!

Making tomato soup is an easy way to make a delicious, healthy dinner for the whole family. The bright colors of the vegetables will be sure to catch your kids' attention, making them eager for mealtime! With only a few ingredients and minimal prep work, how could you not give this recipe a try?

For an extra special touch, top the soup with a dollop of creamy yogurt or grated Parmesan cheese. It's sure to be a hit! Enjoy!

Carbonara Pasta

Carbonara pasta is a delicious and easy-to-prepare dinner for kids. To make it, simply cook the spaghetti according to the instructions on the package. Meanwhile, fry some pancetta or bacon in a pan with a bit of olive oil until it's golden brown and crispy. Beat two eggs in a bowl and stir in some grated Parmesan cheese, salt and pepper. Once the spaghetti is cooked, drain it and transfer to the pan with the pancetta or bacon. Add in the egg mixture and stir everything together over medium heat until everything is nicely combined and the eggs have cooked through. Serve hot with a sprinkle of extra Parmesan on top! The carbonara pasta is a healthy and delicious meal for kids that can be prepared in just a few minutes. Enjoy!

Beef Burger

Making a healthy and easy beef burger dinner for kids is a breeze. Start by prepping the ingredients: dice one small onion, add 500g good-quality beef mince, one egg and 1 tablespoon of vegetable oil to a large bowl. Mix all the ingredients together until fully combined. Form four equal patties from the mixture and place on a plate. Heat some oil in a large non-stick pan over medium heat, then add the beef patties and cook for 3-4 minutes each side or until cooked through. While the beef patties are cooking, cut burger buns in half and lightly toast them in the oven or on a griddle pan. When ready, top the buns with a beef patty and your choice of toppings. We recommend sliced tomato, beetroot, horseradish sauce, mayonnaise, ketchup and a handful of iceberg lettuce or rocket/watercress for a nutritious burst of greens. Serve up and enjoy! Your kids will love this tasty and healthy beef burger dinner. Bon appétit!

Sweet Potato Casserole

For an healthy, easy dinner that kids will love, try preparing a sweet potato casserole. Preparing this delicious dish is simple and straightforward- all you need are 4 cups of peeled and cubed sweet potatoes, 2 large eggs beaten, 1/2 cup white sugar, 1/2 cup of milk, 4 tablespoons butter softened, 1/2 teaspoon vanilla extract, and 1/2 teaspoon salt.

Start by preheating your oven to 350 degrees Fahrenheit. Then mix together the cubed sweet potatoes, eggs, sugar, milk, butter and spices in a large bowl until they are combined evenly. Pour the mixture into a greased 9x13 inch baking dish and spread it evenly across the bottom. Bake in preheated oven for 40 minutes until potatoes are tender, and then let the casserole cool before serving.

For an extra special touch, you can top off your sweet potato casserole with crushed pecans or marshmallows before baking. Enjoy this easy and delicious dinner with your family and friends. With its creamy texture, sweet taste and easy-to-make preparation, it will be a hit with everyone!

Bon Appetite!

Enjoy! :)

Thank you

We hope you enjoyed our book

As a small family company your feedback is very important to us.

Please let us know how you like our book.

9 783755 113157